My Soul Does Sing: "ALL IS WELL..."
(A Divine Visitation)

Experienced and narrated by
Shirlylou

xulon
PRESS

My Soul Does Sing: "ALL IS WELL..."
by Shirlylou

Printed in the United States of America

ISBN 9781615797592

www.xulonpress.com

Table of Contents:

This narrative is dedicated to my son, Wil, with whom the experience was shared, and whose personal faith in Christ helped to carry him as we walked together through a dark, perilous tunnel. Remembered also are the many others who have walked through serious trauma, and ultimately realized they were enabled to find victory through the faithful care of our Divine Creator, knowing that every need was taken care of at the Cross through the suffering of Jesus Christ.

I humbly thank those who fasted and prayed for Wil and me, gave us financial and emotional support, and Dick and Evelyn Armstrong, who went out of their way often to help. I cherish the closeness we felt to my daughter Pennie and family, my sibblings, and other relatives and friends.

Thanks to my teaching collegue and sister in Christ, Armenia Hawkins, who supported the completion of this book and walked with me as I tried to find the courage and direction to complete the publication.

May the Holy Spirit continue to inspire and direct my life and the life of others, and may God ever receive glory.

Preface:

To be aware of angelic protection and sense the presence of God are experiences commonly available to the Christian. Seeing angels is also a part of life available to Christians, though not as frequently experienced. However, the greatest, most fulfilling phenomenon in my life, second only to finding Christ as my Savior, was when God transported me to another time, another place, and then providentially spoke.

Chapter 1:

DAILY ROUTINE DISRUPTED...

As I was settling into bed, preparing for a night's rest, my thoughts were focused on classes to be taught in the morning, and how God had faithfully and intricately weaved direction into my life. Each time during the presence of stress, challenge, or trauma of any sort, God's Grace and Goodness were in abundance. During times of rest, His loving care would effervescently flow. Thanking Him for His faithfulness, I turned out the light and closed my eyes.

As sleep began to envelope me, the ringing of the phone broke the night's silence. A phone call at this time was not unusual, as both of my children would often call to check on me. They seemed to have become rather protective since their father had gone on to be with the Lord, and increasingly guarding after I experienced widowhood for the second time.

As I cheerfully answered the phone, the voice on the other end said, "Mother, there is blood in my eyes and I can't really see. I called you because I found the one key to push to call you. I can't see to find my work number, and I can't see to call anyone else."

This call had turned out to be extremely disturbing! My heart raced as my mind flew back to the years of Wil's childhood. We were often astounded as we witnessed what a "calm, cool head" he had in any given situation. Again, even in this situation, though I heard and felt anxiety in his voice, I knew that it was because of his normal "calm" that he was able to think what to do.

This was a tough shock for me to handle. Since I had no spouse, Wil was my covering and counselor many times when I needed a man's understanding or wisdom, especially during the process of making a serious decision. At this moment he was the son in need and I was the parent who was supposed to be able to help! What made this situation worse was that I was in Texas and he was in Colorado. A lump formed in my throat. The usual sense of peace was greatly shaken. I felt helpless being such a great distance away from him.

We prayed and then talked for a little while, and he assured me he would feel the keys and call my sister and brother-in-law who lived nearly 20 miles from him.

Over the next ten days while I was completing a teaching agreement, his uncle and aunt took him to various doctors, specialists, etc. It was extremely difficult for me to stay focused on the classes while knowing that each day Wil was struggling. Where were the answers to these many questions surrounding this syndrome: "What has caused this happening? Can it at least be helped? Is it permanent? Will the cause effect the body in other ways? ? ? ?" It seemed that my mind raced with questions.

By now, Wil was holding on to someone's shoulder to follow direction when walking. The doctors were rather puzzled, able only to question the possibility of diabetic retinopathy. This possibility did not seem reasonable as they checked him and ran tests. With prudence, Wil had taken care of himself; He had eaten within the realm of what was acceptable, closely monitored his blood sugar, exercised faithfully, etc. To add confusion to the many questions, none of the doctors had seen a patient who experienced sudden blindness in one eye, certainly not both simultaneously, caused by diabetic retinopathy. This is a progressive condition and is usually treated during the progression. There seemed to be no explanation; there simply were no answers.

About three weeks before this phenomenon, Wil had committed to go with me when I returned to minister in Zambia and South Africa the summer of 2008. Now he could not see, was having difficulty doing much for himself, and the reality of the trip to the continent of Africa seemed to be rapidly fading.

My teaching assignment was completed, and the new one was to begin after Thanksgiving. Little did it register at the time: The possibility of my returning to teach after

Thanksgiving was gravely thin, but my mind seemed to overlook that truth. Until being with Wil and seeing him in person, I remained in denial of the depth of the seriousness of the situation.

Chapter 2:

NEW DEMANDS, OSTACLES TO FAITH...

The night before we headed for Colorado, a pastor called to say that as he prayed for Wil, God showed him that Wil was a modern day Job. As he remained faithful to God, everything lost would be restored and multiplied in blessings. Another friend asked me, "Can you look anyone in the eye and say that you know God is ever faithful, no matter what takes place? Can you, without doubt, voice with unfaltering faith that you trust God to meet all of your needs?" My answer to him was simply, "I think so." In many cases, thinking is definitely NOT sufficient. We must fully know!

November 16, 2007, my daughter, her family, and I set out for Colorado to spend our planned Thanksgiving holiday together. The drive there included moments of spontaneous laughter, interesting sights, and fun fellowship. It is always a special pleasure to spend time with grand-children, and with them there was eager anticipation of playing in the snow, going up into the mountains, and seeing other relatives coming in for the holidays. Yet, deep within, and heavy on my heart, were those unanswered questions concerning the well-being of my son.

We arrived at my sister's where Wil was staying while waiting for us to take him back to his home. I felt a stunning shock as if electricity had passed through my body! He had lost a measureable amount of weight, and there was lack of color in his skin. He truly looked sick. I secretly tried to convince myself that through motherly concern, I was imagining his look of illness. However, my daughter Pennie also privately voiced her concern. Her brother simply did not look like her brother.

Back at his home, purchased just a few months before this incident, he defended the weight loss and skin color, stating that he had been unable to get out and exercise. Although his defense did not seem to be the real answer, we did not confront him with that issue. We just knew that he looked ill.

During the week my daughter's family was with Wil and me, we began noticing that Wil's hearing seemed to be lessening. He would ask repeatedly what was said, turn the TV volume louder, and often nelect to answer when addressed by one of us. Also, during this time I was dealing with serious panic. I was truly fearful of driving in Denver traffic, did not know where to take Wil when the need would rise, and felt entirely inadequate to "carry the load." This is called, "trying to be self-sufficient, and walking in lack of faith." I was trying to carry a load which should never have been mine, but should have been released to the One Who cares for His children. When we carry that which is not for us to carry, we eventually break. My time of breaking soon came.

While my daughter's family was still in Colorado with Wil and me, I tried to observe the roads we took to arrive at various destinations, with my daughter driving her vehicle and my son-in-law driving Wil's. Both of my children have always been blessed with a good sense of direction, and at this time, it appeared that God had blessed Wil with a gifted sixth sense to know where he was and when to turn which direction, although he was blind. Truly this was a wonder. Now, after that week, when Wil and I were left alone with me in the driver's seat, he could usually tell me if I missed a turn, was going the wrong direction, just where the next turn should be, etc. Faithful as He is, God met us at this need and had equipped us for what lay ahead! Yet, somehow, while Pennie and family were there, Wil's God-given gift did not seem to register hope to me.

My daughter's family was preparing to return to their home in Texas, and I fell apart! I broke! I cried because the pizza dropped to the floor when removed from the oven; I cried because now I would be the one responsible for the driving in busy Denver traffic where I did not know the way; I cried because now I would be my son's care-giver and felt totally inadequate for that position;

I cried simply because I seemed to have forgotten how to do anything else!

What had happened to my life of prayer, praise, and worship? Although my family were all telling me that Wil and I would be okay, my body seemed to break out in rigorous trembling as my heart quivered in fearful shock! When we let fear overtake us, we lose the strength of our weapons for daily warfare as given in Ephesians 6.

Chapter 3:

DIFFERENT DAY, DIFFERENT CHALLENGE...

My sister and brother-in-law drove us to Wil's eye specialist a few times after I was left there alone with Wil, and then dear, old-time friends from the 1970's began traveling from Boulder to help us with the eye appointments. I managed to drive for any other need while still aided by Wil's God-given gift of location awareness. (After five months, I had to begin driving Wil to the eye doctor. That was a terrifically challenging feat for me! I would take medicine to help curb nausea, just so I could get Wil to the doctor without having to stop along the way.)

December 1, 2007, I drove Wil to the ER because he was in wrenching pain. He had fallen by tripping over his dog because of lack of sight, and the fall had resulted in a dislocated shoulder. Wil had been an extremely active individual and had experienced previous dislocations. Previous experience enabled him to put his shoulder back in place, but he could not seem to rise above the pain. After x-rays, the doctor sent him home with a very strong dose of pain medication and instructions to see his family doctor on Monday, suggesting his doctor set up physical therapy.

On Monday, Wil began fighting nausea. When his doctor saw him, it was determined that the pain medicine prescribed to him in the ER was too strong. Thus, the doses were decreased, and Wil was sent home with an appointment to begin physical therapy on Thursday.

Tuesday and Wednesday we stayed at home, trying to relax. I tried to focus on God's Goodness, and along with spending time in praise and worship and reading Scripture, I watched old movies with Wil. These were movies with which Wil was very familar and could entertain himself (and me) by quoting the next phrase of one of the characters. However, by now his hearing was essentially gone, so he wanted the volume quite high. I would sit with my ears covered and he would strain to hear.

Although God was pouring love on me, and I knew He was present, seeing my once strong, active son now weak and in much physical and emotional pain, created an almost inpenatrable barrier to peaceful rest. Yet, God never moved away from either of us.

As a child, I used to listen while my mother read tales of Polyanna. Recalling that there really can be something positively good out of every situation, and as the Holy Spirit brought back to my remembrance, "Goodness," I began again realizing that Wil's and my cups were half-full rather than half-empty, and I determined to expect good to come out of all of this trauma. (It was certainly helpful the next night, Thursday night, to have already made that determination!)

Wednesday night and Thursday, Wil's nausea problem became more severe. By Thursday afternoon around 4:00, the doctor sent Wil back to the ER, ordering two bags of fluid through an IV, expecting that when they were completed, he would then return home. By now the only way to communicate with Wil was to loudly talk directly into his ear, thus, speaking right at his ear, I explained why we needed to return to the hospital ER.

A couple of ER personnel recognized us from the visit five days earlier, and commented on how sorry they were that he was still having some kind of trouble. There was nothing for Wil to do but to lean back on the ER bed and wait, and wait, and wait...

Chapter 4:

CAUGHT TOTALLY OFF GUARD...

Eventually, after what seemed to be many hours, but was really about one hour, a nurse informed me that Wil would be there for a couple more hours to complete the IV of fluid to hydrate him, get some extra blood work done, and then he would be dismissed to return home.

Now I began to think that surely I would be taking Wil back home, he would begin feeling better, we would be seeing the eye specialist, there would be answers to help him recover, and Wil would be back to work soon. I really did look for the glass to be half full, and expected it to be filling to the brim.

WHOA! I was completely unprepared for what came next: The ER doctor, whose appearance had not been noticed until this moment, came into the cubicle, looked at me, looked at Wil, and then as he stared at me he said, "I can't let your son go home. He has leukemia, and I don't know how long he will live." Without hesitation, he turned, walked out of the area, and was not to be seen by me again.

I felt as if every drop of blood was leaving my body. I could not discuss this with Wil at the moment, and because the doctor was not talking loudly into Wil's ear, Wil had no clue what had been said. There was no one in the room with whom to talk. I staggered out to the nurses' station only to be smiled at and walked around, as if I were an obstacle in the middle of the road. The nursing staff went on about their business. Did anyone have anything to say to me? Did anyone even know what I had been told? Was there anyone who cared? I somehow managed to convey to Wil that he needed to stay in the hospital that night, and managed to call my sister so my brother-in-law could come get Wil's little dog. Oh, sure, there were relatives to call, especially my daughter and family now back at home in Texas, and our very special friends in Boulder, but somehow, it did not matter who talked with me on the phone, I just could not release the tears quickly enough! What would I do now? What could Wil do?

I needed help to totally focus and lean on God.

How could I explain all of this to Wil and still be encouraging? Where had my inner strength gone? I felt as if life was slipping away, fading out of reach, and there was no one to cross over this treacherous, rocky road with me or to help keep me from falling down the steep side of the mountain.

Suddenly, flashing before me was the time in my life when my sixteen-year-old daughter lay ill in the hospital facing possible surgery, a surgery which would prevent her from ever conceiving children. During that time when I cried out to God, He told me that not only would He help me climb the mountain, He would carry me up and over it. Our daughter did not have surgery, and God has blessed her with three wonderful children.

Then I was taken back to the scene of my husband of almost thirty-seven years, my children's father, lying in the hospital as life was fading from his body and he went to be with Christ forever. I remember asking God, "What are we, You and I, going to do now? Will You pour strength into me? What am I doing and where am I going?" God was faithful. Yet, as my mind came back to Wil, the tears continued to flood.

Abruptly I was moved to the scene of walking into my Texas home where my second spouse of just over one year lay on the living room floor unconscious, suffering with convulsions. Struggling while in shock, I managed to call for an ambulance. In the hospital, with my daughter's help and surrounded by friends, I released John to Jesus.

Now, I was again back in Colorado in the ER with the stinging words of the doctor: "...and I don't know how long he will live."

When Wil was taken out of the room for some type of testing, I grappled my way along the hall trying to find an empty room with a Bible. Had I known we would be staying at the hospital, I would definitely have had my own Bible, my Sword, with me! The empty room was found, but no Bible.

I stumbled into the room, fell into a chair, and did more of what I had been trying to suppress: I sat and cried! This time, surprisingly however, crying seemed to provide a sense of relief. As the tears flooded my cheeks and drenched my clothing, I tried to block out the tottering emotion of devastation. For a fleeting moment, I sensed that my tears were precious to Jesus. I was reminded of the Scripture that said something about our tears are put in a bottle. I felt a hint of comfort in remembering that Scripture, though I did not remember exactly where it was or even the exact wording.

There have been times of sorrow, confusion, or pain during which I have asked God to hold me. This certainly was one of those times. I imagined myself sitting in God's lap, (although the Bible says God is a Spirit), in a large, over-stuffed rocking chair. I began crying out to God, my Heavenly Father: "Oh, God, I need to hear from You. Please, just let me hear from You. I need some comfort and assurance. I need You!"

Chapter 5:

ASSURANCE FROM GOD...

Aware that I was in God's care, I realized that He was taking me away from the hospital to some other place in another time. God transported me into the Old Testament days of when the prophet Elisha ministered to the people. I faintly remembered something about a woman whose son had died and she confessed faith as she looked for either Elisha or Elija to pray for her son, but I could not remember which prophet it was, and I knew few details. In that moment God greatly expanded what I knew and filled me with a new realm of understanding.

It dawned on me that somehow I had been invisibly plopped into the home of the Shunamite woman. I heard her discuss the idea of building a room for the prophet Elisha. Her husband did not even question, but honored her wishes as she honored the man of God. God showed me her humility and unquestioning, (like the faith of a child) acceptance of God's Holiness and the validity of Elisha.

Suddenly, I saw the little boy with whom God had blessed the woman and her husband through answering Elisha's prayer. I felt the pain as I heard the young boy hold his head and cry, "My head! My head!" (1) I could see the mother affectionately caressing the boy as she held him on her lap. I saw the life go out of the boy as he died on her knees at noon.

This woman, though vexed, did not hesitate, but she took the boy into the room built for Elisha, laid him on Elisha's bed, and closed the door as she left. Laying him on Elisha's bed was her first step of faith during this trial.

God let me hear her as she called to her husband working in the field, asking for an ass and one of the men go with her. Even as he questioned why, she stated, "It shall be well," and just confirmed that she needed to find the prophet. (2)

God let me see that although this woman had the opportunity to cry and fall into her husband's arms and state that their son was dead, she chose to stand in faith and look beyond the circumstance. She was really saying to her husband, "That's okay, don't worry, go ahead and get your work done because this issue is being resolved."

God took me right along beside the woman as she rode the ass. I could hear her say to herself, "It is well..." It was as if she were praising God and assuring herself all in the same breath. I felt the dust from the road on my feet and smelled it as I breathed. The periodic "snort" of the ass was authentic as it carried her to the prophet.

Elisha and Gehazi were up ahead talking. I could feel the atmosphere of gentle, yet firm authority coming from Elisha, and I felt like I wanted to reach out and grab his arm. I wanted to absorb some of the anointing, the deeply embedded confidence and God-ness I sensed in Elisha. I expected Elisha to immediately know why the woman had come, but he did not know. This was a good reminder that only God is all-knowing, and we may know things ahead of time, but only what the Holy Spirit reveals to us. A few minutes later Elisha stated that the Lord had hidden this information from him.

Then Elisha sent Gehazi to meet the woman and inquire as to the reason for her visit. Following Elisha's request, Gehazi went out to meet the woman, and asked if things were well with her, her husband, her son. Even at this opportunity to cry about her son, she spoke in faith and said, "It is well." (3) Her determination emitted her faith. I was so engrossed in following her faith that it was not until later I even thought to ask God why she, who was just human like I am, could by-pass the pity parties and continue to stand.

Upon reaching Elisha, this seemingly unbreakable woman broke. She grabbed Elisha's feet and cried out to him with questions. Oh, now I could feel the anger, fear, distrust, lack of faith, and the many emotions most of us go through when facing a crisis. This human reaction of the woman lasted only a moment. The way she dealt with the emotion is the reason for victory in her life: she took all of the emotion straight to the point of help rather than talking about it where there was no help. Later, reading the account in the Scriptures, I read, "She said..." but I heard her speak with her voice raised in volume and quivering as she spoke. (4) In the midst of all of this human emotion, she went right back to her focus: the goal of having Elisha come pray. She did not waver from her request for Elisha to come pray. God showed me that we are to remain steadfast in what we know as truth and not be influenced by what is seen or heard around us. So very often, the circumstance is not what makes the result in our lives, it is our response to the circumstance.

Although Gehazi was sent with Elisha's rod, the woman clung to Elisha's feet, declaring that she would not return home without

Elisha. There was no lack of determination with this woman. She held firmly to her faith!

The tears again streamed down my cheeks. "Why was this woman able to stay so single-minded? Why could she cry out to Elisha with her need while still able to declare, 'It is well'? Where did that undying faith originate? How? Why? Please, God, show me!"

To begin with, she had faith in God, and was spiritually sensitive enough that she recognized Elisha as a prophet, a man of God. She honored him as he served God through ministering to the people.

Next, God showed me that just like the way she gave the prophet full reign to move about and live in the room her husband built for him, we are to give totally of ourselves to God, allowing the Lord to freely live within us, and we are to responsively hear the Holy Spirit as he comforts and directs us.

Furthermore, this woman walked in humility, content with where she lived and what she had. Although Elisha offered to get her husband a position with the king or army captain, she declined. She sought no status or extra material wealth. Her joy, contentment, status, all came from her faith in God and not something prioritized by man.

Thus, God showed me this woman had taken all preliminary steps leading up to her unfaltering walk in faith. At this point I cried to God, "Please show me if and where a step is missing in my life. I must be able to walk in steadfast faith!"

Unaware of whether Wil was back in the ER cubicle, I followed the woman and Elisha back to the house. I heard nothing on the way except for the woman quietly wispering, "It is well." There was no sound from Elisha other than the wisp of air when he periodically raised his hands toward Heaven to God. The silence was a peaceful, reassuring silence, broken infrequently by the snorting of the ass. This period of time is a blur, but it does not seem that the woman rode the ass returning home. She walked in quick steps. Elisha did not rush, but walked behind her with a large, steady stride.

As we reached the house, there was no greeting to anyone. The woman walked straight up to Elisha's room, leading him to the boy whose body lay lifeless on the bed. The woman did not even hesitate, but immediately left Elisha alone with the boy. I understood how we need to lay our burdens at the Cross and walk away, leaving the work of restoration to Christ. I was totally absorbed in the actions of Elisha. He immediately closed the door, shutting out all disturbance, unbelief, etc. He then prayed to God. I could not hear what he said, but I was aware that his deep voice projected reverence, faith, confidence — all that we each need as we talk with God.

What then took place seemed confounding to me. Elisha moved to the bed and lay on top of the boy with his hands on the boy's hands, his face on the boy's face, etc. There was no speaking during this time, merely one body passing warmth to another body. Amazing! Intriguing! As Elisha arose from the bed, I could see a warm coloring on the boy, but he was not alive!

Though he made no sound, Elisha rose from the bed, left the room, and walked through the house. I did not follow him as he walked, but was aware of him moving about the house. I heard no voices, and it seemed that I just sat, unaware of the boy, unaware of my son, somehow in limbo, in a state of semiconsciousness.

Abruptly, and for only a couple of seconds, I was again aware of being in the room with the boy, with Elisha stretched out on the boy as before. The Scripture tells of the boy sneezing seven times, and then Gehazi is sent to tell the mother to come get the boy. (5) I was only aware that I was "awakened" in the room by hearing the boy sneeze.

Next, I saw the joy of the woman and heard God speaking directly to me saying, "My daughter, for you too, all is well."

"All is well," I heard God telling me! Remembering the words of the doctor, "...and I don't know how long he will live," and just freshly hearing my Heavenly Father assure me that, "All is well," made me feel as though I stood in the middle of a battle field with forces of both sides running at me and pulling against me. Sure enough! We are in a battle in this world. It was reassuring to know Who the Captain of my army was, is, and forever shall be!!!

Just as I was plopped into life in the Bible time of the Shunamite woman and Elisha, I was plopped back into the ER cubicle where Wil was being wheeled to bed. Filled with a mixture of awe, reverence, and impatience, the voice of assurance of the Shunamite woman, and God's gentle, but firm utterance that for me too, "All is well," I looked lovingly, falteringly at my thirty-nine-year-old, seemingly blind and deaf son, the one who was now diagnosed with leukemia and a question of how much time he had left on earth. I begged God to help me remember and hear His voice above all else. I needed to always remember Whose report I would believe.

Chapter 6:

ALL IS WELL...

The stay in the hospital was one of many challenges for both Wil and myself, with moments of humor, pain, questions, and confusion. This was a time during which we each had to go through a variety of emotion, individually standing on our own faith, seeking God for direction and encouragement. Though there was much we shared, Wil's testimony belongs to him, so I will continue to reveal only through my eyes.

I was grateful for visits and phone calls from our friends from Boulder, my sister and brother-in-law who originally took care of him until I could come, my brother, who entertained us with his presence and humor one night in the hospital, and the many other family members and friends who would call or send mail at just the perfect time. The faithfulness of Wil's friend Colby allowed him moments of freedom from the reality of the current circumstance. Colby took him out to eat when he was released from the hospital, and spent time in conversations which allowed Wil to think on things other than what he might be facing. There were those loving pats, prayers, and encouraging words from the Master's Commission students at New Life.

We looked forward to occasional calls from Jeff in Australia, communication from Pastor Sakala in Zambia, and Pastors Craig and Eddie from S. Africa. God truly did send help and support from family and friends scattered around the world. I daily thanked Him for the many blessings as we continued to travel through this rocky, tumultuous road, which sometimes seemed to turn into a dark tunnel.

We did make it back to Wil's home after a number of days in the hospital. The story is still unfolding, and God is never through with us as we continue on this earth. After Wil had major surgery in both eyes, we were counseled to expect little or no sight and certainly no ability of the eyes to focus together.

Remember that God assured me, "All is well." The doctors' care, surgeries, shots directly into Wil's eyes, and eye exercises Wil does, have certainly had an effect, but the greatest impact has been the healing process, made possible because of Christ at the Cross. We have been given support from friends and family in many states, along with Australia, Poland, Zambia, and South Africa. There have been fastings and prayer vigils for us. Though Wil was given minimal hope concerning sight, he now has been released to drive, using wisdom and trying to drive only where he may be comfortable. (probably good advice for many of us) He is able to again work out at the gym, is regaining weight, strength, muscles, and takes daily chemo tablets, but he is free to adjust his life activities as he is comfortable. His hearing has improved greatly, probably enabling him to hear better than many.

Epilogue:

I am now living back in my home in Texas as Wil adjusts to living on his own in Colorado, asking for help only on the rare occassions when he needs it.

Is God real? Yes, without a doubt! Does God heal? He definitely does! He takes us way beyond what the doctors know or understand. Did God really take me back in time to the Old Testament Bible time as given in II Kings? I can tell you I heard the little boy cry as he held his head, felt and breathed the dust on the road, heard the woman say with firm determination, "It is well," sensed Elisha's calm but firm authority, and absolutely knew that my sovereign God had spoken.

Thinking back on what the pastor said before we left for Colorado, I do see Wil as a modern day Job coming out of the test with multiplied blessings. I believe as he completes his study course at a school near home, he shall be employed in a job superior to what he lost because of this ordeal. God moves us up as we live for Him, and the job which was lost because of the illness, shall be replaced just as Job had more in the end than he did before he was adversely attacked.

In answer to the friend's question, "Yes!" I can look anyone in the eye and with unfaltering confidence state that God is forever faithful!

To help with my son as I left a job in Texas, I took out a mortgage on my home. It will be paid in full within a few years, as will other debt incurred during this time, and the commitment to return to Zambia, South Africa, and Australia, shall be fulfilled. How do I know? I know because I did what had to be done, my life's purpose is to live for and serve God, and God is ever faithful! Will there be any more challenges or hindrances? Ofcourse there will be, but they are not stronger than my God.

My prayer is that you know the God of the universe through His son Jesus Christ, walk in His blessings and peace, and understand that if you place your life in Him, you can trust and know that under any circumstance, God can assure you, too, "All is well!"

"Now the Lord of Peace Himself give you peace always by all means. The Lord be with you all" (6)

Endnotes:

II Kings, Chapter 4, Verse 19
II Kings, Chapter 4, Verse 23
II Kings, Chapter 4, Verse 26
II Kings, Chapter 4, Verse 26
II Kings, Chapter 4, Verse 35
II Thessalonians, Chapter 3, Verse 16

"ALL IS WELL,"

"ALL IS WELL," I heard God say.
How can that be when the doc said,
"He has leukemia and cannot go home today"?

Well, Shadrach, Meshach, and Abed-Nego knew all
was well even in the fiery furnace in a hot pod.
Why? They REALLY knew and trusted God.

Abraham knew all was well when God said to sacrifice
Isaac, his son.
Why? Because he knew God well, walked in faith, and to
God he knew to always run.

Moses knew all was well when he chose to suffer with his
own people of God.
Why? He knew God personally, and he was granted power
through using his rod.

All was well when the walls of Jericho fell.
Why? Joshua led the people around 7 times, just as God's
instructions did tell.

David knew all was well when the great giant he fought.
That's because in the field watching sheep and singing to God, the lessons of bravery were taught.

There were women of the Bible who knew all was well.
In fact, men looked to Deborah for leadership, because God's
wisdom they knew she would tell.

Yet, with the many examples of those who knew all was well,
during my time of trauma, God took me to the Shunamite woman and told me: "My daughter, for you, too, ALL IS WELL!"

You see, even though her son lay on the bed and to others he was dead, she kept her faith renewed.
She stayed focused on Elisha's anointing, and to God's work through the prophet her vision stayed glued.

So... When the doctor's report left little hope for my son, God told me, as the Shunamite woman understood, for me too: "ALL IS WELL," FOR THROUGH FAITH IN GOD WE HAVE ALREADY WON!

(Poem inspired by the Holy Spirit, as I thought back on this yet incomplete journey, before my son was released to be on his own. February, 2009)

CPSIA information can be obtained
at www.ICGtesting.com
Printed in the USA
FSOW01n1909230415
6683FS

9 781615 797592